BLUFF YOUR WAY IN PUBLISHING

DOROTHY M. STEWART

RAVETTE BOOKS

Published by Ravette Limited
3 Glenside Estate, Star Road
Partridge Green, Horsham
West Sussex RH13 8RA
(0403) 710392

First published 1987
Revised 1992

Series Editor – Anne Tauté

Cover design – Jim Wire
Printing & Binding – Cox & Wyman Ltd.
Production – Oval Projects Ltd.

The Bluffer's Guides are based on
an original idea by Peter Wolfe.

CONTENTS

Getting into Publishing   7
  Good Names for Publishing   7
  Preparation for Publishing   8
  The Publishers   9

The Publishing Process   14
  Editorial   15
  Production   19
  Sales and Marketing   24
  Publicity   24
  Reps and Sales Conferences   29
  Distribution   32
  Dealing with Booksellers   33

Playing the Game   37
  Authors   37
  Agents   40
  Auctions   41
  Contracts   42
  Foreign Rights   44
  Book Fairs   48
  How to Get Started on Your Own   52
  What to Publish   53
  Packaging   55
  How to be Acquired   56

Glossary   58
  General Terms   58
  Editorial, Print and Production Terms   59
  Marketing Terms   61
  Rights Terms   43

For ideas, information and inspiration, grateful thanks
and acknowledgement is given to:

Anthony Blond
Andrew Stuck
Bill Swainson
Bart Ullstein

INTRODUCTION

Anyone can become a publisher. Unlike the sort of people you bump into on a normal day – your plumber, accountant, hairdresser, psychiatrist – a publisher though he (and increasingly she) may consider himself professional, needs no formal qualifications whatsoever.

Once upon a time, birth, wealth and an instinct for backing winners made all the difference. Now, all you need is an Apple Mac and a passion for high stakes. You don't even need money, because printers still have a sweet regard for those who call themselves publishers and will usually give 60 days credit to anybody who sets themselves up in the business of publishing. For 60 days in this business read 6 months.

Publishing is a delightful way for young persons of independent means to occupy their spare time. Whether you wish to fill in time between university and higher things or have your sights on a 'career', publishing has one certain benefit: it is never dull. It is that delightful anomaly, a gentleman's occupation, a business without the stigma of trade.

'People go into publishing because of the excitement', according to the Association of American Publishers. It is seen as a glamorous occupation by people outside. These are the ones who have little connection with it. However, some people in publishing are glamorous (for example Mark Barty-King, described by *The Sunday Times* as 'designer-clad ... his six feet four of even teeth and crunching handshake matched by a regularity of features that makes Robert Redford look faintly deformed'). The rest are a mixed bag of eccentrics, earnest types and enthusiasts.

5

The tyro (old-fashioned words are cherished by publishers) would be wise to steer a middle path, not taking the business too seriously.

To break into publishing, a certain amount of information is essential. There is no point trying for a position at Walker Books for example, if your interest is engineering, or applying to The Women's Press if you are male. Publishing is a sub-culture with its own language, ethos, and dramatis personae. Do not be daunted. The hallmark of the successful publisher is that he or she is a generalist, a renaissance man/woman or dilettante. In other words, a bluffer. With the help of this book, you too can join this select band.

GETTING INTO PUBLISHING

By far the most efficient method of getting in to publishing is to inherit a publishing house. This saves the effort and expense of scanning the 'Creative and Media' pages, fighting a friendly newsagent for *The Bookseller*, and the tedium of attending job interviews. If you can marry into it, or know someone who is already in the business, so much the better.

For those without such connections, all is not lost. Job turnover is high and many vacancies vanish as redundancies, but there *are* jobs around especially if you are prepared to start 'at the bottom'. You will be glad to know that suitability for this position, and the length of time you stay there, depends less on your skills and qualifications than on how you 'fit into' the miniature world that is the publishing company. This fit derives to a considerable degree from your pedigree, the shape of your chin, and your name.

Good Names for Publishing

In-depth research has shown that you are more likely to secure a job in publishing, and subsequent success, if your name is included in the following list:

Simon, Adrian, Jeremy, Charles, Mark, Patrick, Leo, Ant(h)ony, Tim, Dominic, Robert, Nigel, Ian (or Ion), Alexander, Roland, Christopher, Nick, Malcolm, Peter.

Sarah, Victoria, Imogen, Fiona, Julia, Pandora, Liz, Philippa, Fenella, Sally, Lucinda, Pamela, Charlotte, Selina, Caroline, Philomena, Ursula, Penelope, Susan.

Your surname is also important. If you can't manage a hyphen, as for example Hodder-Williams, Gordon-Walker or Chadwyck-Healey, or a double barrel without a hyphen e.g. Hely Hutchinson, try for something solidly British like Bell. Failing that be unashamedly exotic, taking your inspiration from Callil, Attallah, Bagherzade, Piatkus, Deutsch, Rosenthal, Reinhardt, Zomboroy-Moldovan, du Sautoy or Fuglewicz.

Preparation for Publishing

Some publishing companies train their staff, but with little enthusiasm for fear of:

a) giving the lowlier ones ideas above their station

b) providing the bright ones with some real information, or

c) showing up the intellectual dullness of the prefect and director levels.

Training is likely to be for the job you were doing two years' ago. But don't spurn the opportunity. If it's an outside course, you can make contacts and if it's in house, you have the chance to ingratiate yourself with the powers-that-be.

Pay and Rations

In publishing an independent income is a good thing. Salaries are considered unnecessary. This is because publishing is prestigious. Once upon a time, people were prepared to work for free, or for pittances, just to get their foot on the publishing ladder. Nothing has changed.

Skills

Publishing likes to think of itself as an intellectual profession, attracting the brightest minds from the best universities. If you desire to play this game, you must have a degree, so make sure it is Oxbridge and something unlikely, for example Cybernetics or Ethnic Studies. A degree in English Literature is the surest route to the exit.

Do not under any circumstances reveal that you "simply love books." Nobody in publishing loves books. Those that did, got out.

The Publishers

It is important to choose your niche. Publishers, unlike black cats, are not all alike. You need to know the difference between the far-flung Pan-Macmillan empire and the Random Century federal form; between Sinclair-Stevenson's Eton-and-Trinity type publishers to the upper classes and André Deutsch's string-saving but profitable fierce bookmanship; between the lean and mean style of the small independents, and the aesthetic daring of Faber and Faber.

Now that most recognized publishers are owned by someone else there is little point in keeping up with who owns whom. All that is necessary is to be able to distinguish the predators from the prey. Maxwell is no longer to be feared, Murdoch (HarperCollins/ Unwin Hyman/Thorsons/News International) is. Other big game hunters are S. I. Newhouse (Random Century/Ballantine), Pearson (Penguin/Longman/ Hamish Hamilton/Addison-Wesley, etc.), and Reed International (Heinemann/Octopus, etc.).

It may help to categorize publishers in a number of ways, such as:

1. those who receive reverential mention in *The Bookseller*, and
2. those who often make not so respectfully the columns of the *Evening Standard* diary and *Private Eye*.

The first tend to be profitable; the second tend to be better known for their losses and their social connections. A strange peccadillo of publishing is to decry those who make money, saying they're the kind who never read a book. Take heed for those who do this, don't.

A further useful categorisation is into Gentlemen and Players. Gentlemen are the establishment/institution type houses with a self-conscious sense of history, and an adherence to systems built into their very fabric. These companies publish, produce and talk about 'books'.

The Players are the newcomers, the paperback houses, and those driven by industrial conglomerates, where the civilising veneer is very thin. You can identify them rapidly and easily by their use of the word 'product' for what they publish. It would appear that their business is no different from the producers of other products, like butter or bars of soap.

It has been suggested that the new names in publishing are:

a) not English
b) not Gentlemen, and
c) not publishers.

The greatest fun is to be a Player in a house of Gentlemen, but not the other way round.

Location

Before the War, Paternoster Row (or near it) was the only possible place in which to have an office. But since the move of established publishers – e.g. OUP, Macmillan and Longman – (to Oxford, Basingstoke and Harlow respectively), Weidenfeld (south of the Thames) and HarperCollins (to Hamersmith) it no longer matters where you are: in town, out of town, or half-way to America.

You have a choice of office style:

a) Dickensian cubby-holes close to strip-tease joints in Soho (e.g. Bloomsbury)

b) panelled shabby cosiness (Gollancz, Souvenir)

c) refurbished tranquil elegance, overlooking Bedford Square (Hodder & Stoughton, Thames & Hudson)

d) neon-lit atria, complete with designer plants and static carpets (Penguin, HarperCollins, Random Century)

e) utterly eccentric – a piano factory (Duckworth), church crypt (Sheldon), art-deco tyre warehouse (Octopus).

d) your own back room.

The Name

In publishing everything is in the name. If you want to start your own company and you happen to have a nice name like Ricketson Hat, use that, which is memorable, and not The Eland Press, which is not. If your name is not euphonious, change it. Jonathan

Cape did. So did Allen Lane. Try to think objectively about this. Some didn't, for example David & Charles, who despite their traditional connection with railways, sound like a ladies' hairdresser.

Generally speaking, people who start in publishing with an imprint called the something Press, usually fail. There are a few 'presses' still in business, but Companies House is a depository of dusty failures with this title.

Logos and Imprints

Publishers like to be recognised by their logos (colophons to the more traditional) which they stick on the spines of their books – except for Bloomsbury who has Diana the Huntress uncomfortably straddling the spine. They work terribly hard on these, but the evidence is that the reading public (all three of them and all living in Hampstead) do not really notice. In general, readers hate bookshops organised by publisher and simply want books first in subject order then in author order, with the exception perhaps of Penguin, Virago and Mills & Boon.

What Publishers Publish

There is a general belief that the number of titles each year is excessively large. Despite this, publishers go on increasing output (67,704 in 1991, and rising). Many tend toward the scattergun approach – publishing a wide variety of books in the hope that enough will sell in sufficient numbers to justify the gamble.

Others have one main brand on which they are heavily dependent, e.g. Beatrix Potter at Frederick

Warne (its value recognised in the c.£6 million take-over by Penguin). If you don't like the brand, don't join the company.

Fiction:

Romance – Historical, Hospital, Gothic, Bodice Rippers, Slavers, Cliterature.

Thrillers – Crime, Spy, Disaster, Horror, Porn.

SF/Fantasy – New World, Swords and Sorcery, Hubbard's World.

Boy's Own – War, Westerns, Adventure, Voyeurism.

Non-Fiction:

General – Biography, Entrepreneurial Autobiography, How To, Sport, Hobbies, Green Issues, War, Sex.

Reference – Dictionaries, Directories, Encyclopaedias.

Educational – School, Academic, Professional, Scientific, Technical, Medical.

Alternative – Pop, Politics, Health, New Age, Sex.

Children – All the above for the under twelves.

THE PUBLISHING PROCESS

Most publishers are in a permanent state of slippage. No working day ever achieves an absolute advance. This is because most days are taken up with preventing disaster and righting wrongs. Printing machinery breaks down, photocopiers pack up, manuscripts are mislaid – and always, always, authors are late.

To deal with this, the industry has developed a full supporting cast, each of whom contributes something to help (or hinder) the process.

Depending on the company, these will have different titles. In some, everyone is an executive, in others, a director or manager, e.g. Chief Executive, Sales Manager, Rights Director. But in general, you will encounter four main functions: Editorial, Production, Sales & Marketing, and Distribution – although the last three are not really considered part of publishing. Note the absence of Accounting or Finance.

It is important when considering these functions, to remember that many people in a particular position have first been something else – e.g. Rep promoted to Marketing Manager, Secretary to Editor. Indeed, some of them are all things at once (see How to Get Started on Your Own). However, the reverse also applies, and many who have large aspirations find themselves after many years, still sending out review copies.

Also remember that anyone who describes their work as being 'in publishing' will almost certainly be:

a) underpaid
b) undervalued
c) not an Editor (the only ones who consider themselves real publishers).

14

Editorial

There are two kinds of Editor: Commissioning (or 'sponsoring') and Desk/Copy or Production Editors.

Commissioning Editors

These are the people who decide whether a work will be published. Mentors, minders, sharp business people, they are the prefects of the publishing world.

Commissioning editors travel, and have company cars – Cavaliers or Escorts, the occasional Golf. They are seldom in the office, but they are extremely busy. They very often 'work at home', supposedly avoiding interruptions. They're seldom with an author but they know lots of other commissioning editors and all the appropriate agents. Some of the books they describe as 'my books' – they are vicariously prolific this way.

You can be one of two types of commissioning editor:

1. The proactive editor, or
2. The reactive editor.

As the first, you have to have the idea and you have to find the author. Then you have to enthuse the author enough (here's where the publishing lunch comes in) to write the book the way you want it.

As the second, you take a less active role. The author has the idea and in trying to find a publisher, his or her manuscript finally lands on your desk. Here the effort lies in maintaining poise and cheerfulness in the face of so much dross, and hanging on to the insane optimism that today's post will bring a gem.

Unfortunately, many an author carefully nurtured by a proactive editor will imagine himself to be the second kind of author. This produces much embarrassment as he proffers his deeply cherished but completely unsaleable ideas. Worse still, he may take himself away to a reactive editor and find his ideas taken up and turned into unsaleable books.

Either way, it helps to be schizophrenic. The job requires the skill of a midwife (from an encouraging "yes, you can do it" to the more robust "try harder, push, dammit") matched by the professionalism of the executioner. When the author's new-fledged offering arrives, yours is the thumbs-down that sends it on its way to oblivion.

List-building

The commissioning editor's job is to 'build lists', that is to develop a publishing programme of titles in a given field. You may have inherited a nice backlist, or may face the fruits of a self-indulgent individual, or non-discriminating numbers-merchant, in which case you will need to prune ruthlessly. A good rule of thumb is to declare **o.p.** any books without dramatically good sales by authors who are:

a) trouble
b) friends or relatives of your predecessor.

There are two varieties of backlist:

1. The unsaleable titles you're left with because you printed too many.

2. The ones you make real money from, as you roll out reprints.

Most publishers' backlists satisfy Pareto's Principle (the 80/20 rule): 80% are category (1); 20% are (2).

The older publishers all have gold on their backlists. Macmillan were blessed with Thomas Hardy and *Alice in Wonderland*. Allen & Unwin did well from Tolkien, and Methuen with *Winnie the Pooh*. Faber have done nicely in more ways than one from T. S. Eliot, and John Murray have long benefited from Byron, and more recently, Betjeman.

The secret of editorial success therefore, is one really popular author, who will sell and sell.

If you're lucky, you will have inherited a promising mid-list. This features new authors you want to develop. Otherwise, it's virgin territory.

In choosing new books you should be concerned not so much with readability, as with talkability.

- Can the author talk to the media?

- Will the media talk up the book?

- Can it be talked on to the Booker or Whitbread shortlists?

- Can it be talked on to the Abacus or Black Swan paperback lists?

- Can it be left on the coffee table as a talking point?

And most important of all:

- Will it be talked about enough so that no-one who buys it, need ever read it?

Like all others in publishing, commissioning editors enjoy compliments. But these may be barbed. 'Discriminating' is the accolade most to be desired.

'Caring' may mean you are a soft touch, a walk-over for the bullish agent. 'Creative' may mean:

a) you meddle in the text, design, etc.
b) you're so far out the book is sure to be a flop.

Whatever the case, commissioning editors rarely sully their hands with ink when turning a fair book into a good one, or a good book into an excellent one. This is usually the job of the:

Desk or Production Editor

These are the editorial dogsbodies, the galley slaves without whom the ship will get nowhere. They are the people who turn the tatty illiterate manuscript into clear, lucid prose, sitting neatly on the page, reasonably close to the illustrations. But nobody appreciates this, their names seldom appear in the acknowledgements, and everyone else in the organisation thinks they're a cut above them.

In return, these embittered forgotten heroines (for it is usually women who do this essential job) take the underground route of guerrilla warfare to discharge their grievances. Their much-needed eye for detail may be corroded into nitpicking small-mindedness, as they find ways to get their own back.

They will receive the most cherished manuscript with withering scorn, the most favourite and good-natured author will be turned into a shrieking harpy in rage at editorial queries, and the most important title will mysteriously slip. Such is their power. Recognise the true gold of their contribution, and you will be amply rewarded.

Production

Depending on the organisation, production people may be separate from and in continuous conflict with editors (both sorts). Easily distinguished in a publishing house, these are the harassed individuals who cope with the confusion generated elsewhere. In consequence, they are regarded as a lower form of life.

At heart, they are closer to each other than to any other function, and will close ranks at the least excuse against all outsiders. Otherwise they spend their days in thinly veiled contempt for each other or in open hostility with whoever is to blame for the disasters (pages printed upside down, omitted indexes) and the inevitable slippages. Time, here, is always 'of the essence'.

Quite a few males will be found in production. Their days are spent playing with en rules, fencing with printers, and keeping editors in their place. Their offices are littered with free calendars, desk diaries, lead paperweights, and dummies of various sorts, including printers' representatives. These will seek out production people wherever they are, like blood-hounds following a trail.

Production people are mostly too busy dealing with deadines to visit printers in their lair. This is a pity for printers are very grateful when this happens. If, on your first lunch, you can abstain from alcohol you will amaze and impress, for it is a convention in the printing trade that on publishers' rare visits to their works, customer-publishers should be made legless. You need only do this on the first occasion just to show that you are a hard customer.

Abstinence is especially important when it comes to finalising the print run. Do not get carried away by economies of scale which push the unit cost down to the merest pence. The average print run for a first novel is 1250 and 5000 copies in C-format paperback. Anyone who disputes this is fibbing.

Book Costing

In publishing one golden rule pertains. It is permissible to produce:

- good books that make money (rare)
- bad books that make money (common), and
- good books that lose money (easy)

but the one thing you may never do is produce bad books *and* lose money.

As is to be expected in a basically amateur industry, the financial aspects of book publication are less than sophisticated. Whether you use a calculator, a micro, or a modem linked to the mainframe in the basement, the procedure is the same. The sum done to work out how to price a book, and whether it will be profitable, uses a 'rule of thumb' equation: production cost price (including design, paper, jacket and printing) x 5 for hardbacks, or x 7 for paperbacks, unless you are dealing with an illustrated book, in which case the mark-up is as much as you dare.

Example 1: Hardback book, list price £14.95:

Print Run: 1,250 copies
  less 150 publicity and soiled copies

Value of sales:	£16,445
less 40% discount to bookseller	(£6,578)

Income	(£9,867)

Production cost	(£3,747)
Author's royalties @ 10% of list price	(£1,644)
Gross margin	£4,475

There are two reasons for the hardback book. First it establishes a market for the paperback and second, publishers like it that way. Both reasons collapse when the paperback is published simultaneously.

Example 2: Paperback book, list price £5.95

Print run: 15,000 copies (standard format paperback)
Allow 350 publicity and Rep's 'free' copies.

Value of sales: 14,650 @ £5.95	£87,167
less average 60% discount to bookseller/wholesaler	(£52,300)
Income	(£34,867)

Production cost	(£10,401)
Author's royalty @ 7.5% of list price	(£ 6,537)
Gross margin	£17,929

Note that the publisher makes less than the bookseller. From the gross margin all overhead costs – salaries, heating, lap-tops, trips to New York, etc – must be found, to say nothing of returns. By which time, the publisher is lucky to earn as much as the author.

A reasonably ordinary, high-priced hardback book will break even at around 900 copies. For many titles, breakeven is not reached until the second printing.

Other income can make the vital difference between viability and obscurity for a title. This includes revenue from Book Club deals, serialisation, film, paperback, and foreign rights (*q.v*).

Jackets and Blurbs

The book jacket is felt by publishers to be their 'shop window'. This is not far from the truth since it may be the only shop window the book ever sees. Note that the economy of keeping the same image for both is not only becoming more common, but using the dust jacket wrapped around a paperback will eliminate the need for a hardback altogether.

The jacket also provides the first information that library suppliers, overseas booksellers and provincial booksellers have of a book – and all they may ever see of it. So it matters.

Designs are usually produced on a sort of committee basis and then controlled by the production/art director. You may be sure that whatever is done, it will be unacceptable to the author, and if acceptable to the author, it will be unacceptable to the sales force. Also bear in mind that, although folded round the book, everyone in publishing conceives a design flat, and decides on its appropriateness in this form.

Despite the fact that most publishers can tell you what they are going to publish 18 months to 2 years ahead, work on jackets and blurbs is always begun at the last minute. To help you here are three rules.

1. All the spaces must be filled. You can mention other books on the back panel, or the back flap, but it is not very kind unless they are by the same author and are successful, in which case instead of creating

fresh vibrant prose simply bung in a selection of his/her previous titles (published by your own house, of course).

2. Unless the author is breathtakingly beautiful or bizarre, do not have his or her photograph on the jacket. Explain gently that a print supplied will be used for 'publicity purposes'. (It is understood that this rule will be broken when the author is a bully and/or subsidising publication.)

3. Unless your authors live in exotic parts of the globe, (Outer Hebrides, Tuvalu or Vanuata – Nepal will no longer do) do not mention their habitat. No one ever lost a sale for forgetting to mention that the author lived in a red-brick semi in suburbia.

A successful blurb can be a work of art in its own right, and a well-honed promotional tool. The best prescription for writing one is to drink half a pint of dry sherry on the rocks, shut your eyes, and think like a B-movie producer. A useful device is the shout line. These are mostly found on paperbacks. Often they are quotes from a review of the hardback edition (which, to paperback editors is the main purpose of that process). Sometimes the connections are obvious, sometimes bewilderingly not. For example:

— 'The book that shook the world.'
— 'The astonishing adventures of a merchant, a poet and a captive princess.'
— 'Sex slaves to the Gestapo.'
— 'Economics as if people matter.'
— 'There were boys and there were men.'
— 'The businesses he milked ... the women he made... the men he broke...'

Sales and Marketing

Marketing departments in publishing companies exist but they are a misnomer because:

a) all but about two publishers refuse to worry about the market on the grounds that publishing a book is cheaper than commissioning research, and in any case

b) the editors know best anyway.

Other factors involved are popularly held myths, e.g.

- Every book finds its own level.
- Advertising never sold books in the past, so why start now?
- If the media can devote a large amount of space and air time to pushing books and authors free, why should you pay for it?
- Publishers fear that marketing might turn their 'profession' into an industry and their 'obsession' into product.
- True marketeers earn far too much to consider the publishing business.
- Marketing requires discipline and a clear mind, both qualities sadly lacking in publishing.

Publicity

However many people there are in publicity, there are never enough. The mainstay of the department is an overworked but dedicated female who doesn't go out to lunch, and who stays until long after everyone else has gone, typing labels.

Some publishers resort to using outside aid in the form of freelance publicists, or PR companies. The latter consist of a male, somewhere between 35 and 60 – who may by now have developed a drink problem, and certainly has an aversion to starting the day before 10.30 – supported by a faithful assistant (male or female) who does the work.

The publisher's generally-held view is that if a book succeeds it's because it's a good book, and if it fails, the publicity was wrong. The publicity person's view is that the book sold only because the publicity worked. If it failed, the budget wasn't big enough.

The sales force will always blame the failure upon an inappropriate jacket (a claim for any book) or the fact that it was published too late – an unreasonable excuse because no book has ever been produced on time. (The record holder could be the general title which appeared in eleven seasonal lists prior to its publication; in other words, it was first announced 5 years before it was published, and it was only a translation from German, not a new book. Not surprisingly, this publisher no longer has a general list.)

Publishers generally operate a sliding scale for allocation of promotion money related to the size of the initial printing and the retail price of the book. If the decision is to spend large sums (tens of thousands at least), the book trade is more or less bound to accept the book in quantity. The public is, of course, another matter. Here publicity people have to depend on such methods as:

Radio and TV

Estimates of an author's potential as a public personality, rather than as a writer, should be made early. The best author of all is the confident telegenic one. This has gone so far that some American publishers won't touch book by an author who isn't. Whether or not authors radiate charm and charisma, or are shy, slow of speech and have a squint, make sure they:

a) mention the title from time to time
b) name the publisher at least once
c) carry a copy of the book.

Discussing the features of the book is essential. Chat shows want inside stories and gossip. This was provided par excellence by Jacqueline Susann in the late sixties when promoting *The Valley of the Dolls*. She simply denied that characters in the book were based on real people, and named names generously to show which people the characters were not based on. She denied her way across America and her book sales soared.

Reviews

In Europe and America, book sales are usually in direct relation to the amount of favourable comment they receive. In Britain, this is not always the case. Nobody is quite sure to what extent reviews sell books. However, honourable mention in despatches is part of the ritual of publication.

With a book of literary pretension, pretentious reviews are a must. But the burning question is: are reviewers inter-related, or are they clones, with the occasional rogue mutation?

Very few writers make a real splash – the Amises, father and son, a forgotten Graham Greene, a subject that is unusual or controversial like *Spycatcher*. Second best would be a lead review in the nationals.

If any literary editor complains they have not received a review copy assume that it has either been stolen (a good sign) or sold – and send them another and another. It is better that nationals have twenty copies of the book, than that someone who writes for local dailies in Northern Ireland, deepest Wessex or Ulan Bator has one.

Beware the demand for review copies in a letter typed on a machine dating from 1914 with keys clogged by faded fabric ribbon. This reviewer is not discriminating. He simply asks for any title announced in the trade press. Unfortunately, the coverage he can command is not worth even one copy.

Do not leave allocation of review copies to that nice typist who is so helpful. Oversee the job yourself with the help of someone who has mastery of Pimms PR planner, which lists the names of the people who call the shots reviewing, mentioning, featuring, promoting and/or hyping books.

What the reviews really mean:

authentic — harrowing
harrowing — anatomical
thoughtful — tedious
meticulous — nitpicking
worthy — boring
splendid — long
majestic — endless
lofty vision — pretentious
uncompromising honesty — has dirty bits
a personal view — inaccurate
a good read — of no literary merit

Be very mean with review copies. If the book you are peddling is exceptionally expensive, write to the likely reviewers explaining that this is so and asking if they really want a copy. If the BBC want a copy, charge them. If film producers ask for copies, charge them too and say if they pick up the option you'll refund the money.

Never forget you are not selling the book to the public, you are selling it to booksellers. Far more important than a lead review in a posh paper would be a prediction in a trade paper that you are on to something big. Here the options are:

The Bookseller – The weekly organ of the book trade, read as avidly by publishers as by booksellers, mostly backwards (job ads and bestseller lists apear there). Twice yearly it appears gross and bulging with publishers' advertising. These are the Export numbers. They come out at six monthly intervals because that is how long it takes to get through them.

Publishing News – Essential for gossip, entertainment, and scandal, it is much read in cloakrooms, but not in reception areas. It suffers from a lack of job ads, especially senior appointments, and thus is not as carefully read as its rival.

Prizes for Publicity Purposes

Publishers believe that the ultimate publicity weapon (other than the **launch party**) is the annual **literary award**. Authors can win £21,500 from the Whitbread, £12,500 from the estate of Betty Trask and £8,000 from Smarties. With a total of £29,500, the NCR Book Award for Non-Fiction is Britain's most lucrative book prize. Fast on its heels at £20,000 comes the *Sunday Express* Book of the Year for fiction which is "readable", a concept entirely foreign to publishers who are therefore proscribed from submitting entries. But the one that the publishers covet, the Oscar of literature, is **The Booker**.

This rejuvenated the market in heavyweight hardback fiction. William Golding's 60,000 sales for *Rites of Passage* in around two years was a major breakthrough. Until this, most publishers would have been unsurprised by sales of 2,000 for such a title. The 1989 winner, Kazuo Ishiguro with *The Remains of the Day*, netted 150,000 paperback sales. And the trend continues.

Publishers who don't believe in their authors quite as much as they say they do, catch cold when demand outstrips their meagre print-runs. But others, too enthusiastic, end up remaindering. Those with hardback and paperback imprints are well placed to make a double killing. A Booker winner or also-ran can transform a year's profits.

There is the suggestion that a sort of literary mafia links the judges and the winners, but everybody knows that controversy of this kind is just a ploy to stimulate sales.

Reps and Sales Conferences

Sales conferences are major events in the publishing year. Since they can't be ducked, like so much else in publishing, they galvanise a flagging company into action. In the weeks preceding the great event, catalogues reach proof stage, advance information sheets are run off, covers designed, shout lines invented, and floorshows choreographed.

Sales conferences also serve to remind publishers of their representatives. One of the basic facts of publishing is that a book must first be sold to your sales department (even if they had the idea first); your sales department must then sell it to the reps, who must sell it to the bookseller/wholesaler/W.H. Smith buyer before the purchaser can finally reject it.

There are three main types of sales conference:

1. The Hi-Tech Floor Show
The one that is organised with all the razzamatazz of an American Primary, with special sound and light effects, cabaret performances from star authors, videos, balloons, T-shirts, and even affable appearances by top executives of the company.

2. The Compulsory Holiday in an Isolated Hotel
The one where reps and publishing staff arrive as to a week of purgatory on a health farm. The hot-house atmosphere may concentrate the mind, but frequently only on means of escape. These gatherings often have the queasy ambience of a Christmas family reunion.

3. The Make-Shift Sales Conference
The one held in a room which is always smaller than the number of people it has to accommodate, e.g. the boardroom, or for those without such an august venue, the upstairs of a local pub. Usually quite jolly, it can degenerate into the endless monologue of an embattled editor, sending the reps away in despair as they contemplate unsaleable wares.

Reps themselves come in all shapes and sizes and are generally wise and wonderful*. Here are the more distinctive breeds:

Prototype salesmen, with sharp suits, Samsonite

*We hope to sell this book.

briefcases, and a battery of hard-sell clichés. Relentlessly cheerful as they blast their way through mass market TV tie-ins and awful children's books. Dreaded by booksellers everywhere.

Old warhorses, all male, who have been at the game since the days of incunabula. Occasionally they'll let you know when you've offended against their unwritten code of conduct (such as suggesting they might sell more books).

New style rep, publishing's equivalent of the new style bookseller. Youngish, frequently female, personable, probably with a degree they're keeping quiet, thoroughly professional and setting a new industry standard (to the horror of the old warhorse).

Freelance reps, a law unto themselves. For 10 per cent commission on the turnover in their area, they carry a dozen or so lists of infinite variety. Without the security of a salary, a car or expenses, they are the most energetic people on the circuit.

However, the economics of a freelance rep's life demand that they cream the frontlist to ensure they get the largest amount of commission possible on the least amount of work/time/money. Thus the least saleable (and perhaps the most interesting) books come out of the bag last.

All reps are walking paradoxes. Treat them carefully for they are prone to accentuate the negative and they spend more time with the booksellers than with the publishers who employ them, so the bookseller and his problems may replace you and yours in the rep's affections.

You underestimate reps at your peril. They are often better informed and more literate than anyone else in the business. And, of course, they will always be proven correct in their forecast that 'We'll *never* be able to sell this.'

Distribution

Most publishers are dissatisfied with their book distribution. It is the abiding theme of all ills in the trade and the principal topic at the last four thousand three hundred and twenty five BA conferences. So, unless yours is part of the company, remember that the trick is to switch distributors *before* disillusion has set in – i.e. within the first two years (just as everyone has got used to the new repository).

A good rule in publishing, which as bluffers know is always broken, is to have books in the warehouse two months before publication, and in at least two separate catalogues. These idyllic conditions are never met because of publishers' chronic inefficiency, i.e. books are announced, publicity machines roll, authors go on 'tour', but because the books are not in the warehouse, they are not in the shops.

When books are available, there are two methods of dispatch:

Carriage-free a.k.a **Freight Free** or **Free Freight** – The publisher chooses the method of carriage and pays. Booksellers frequently complain about slowness of delivery. Publishers tend to be an old-fashioned race, and carriage to them tends to have something to do with horses.

Carriage-forward – The bookseller chooses and pays. Not surprisingly, this is altogether faster, but much less frequently used.

Messages pass backwards and forwards from the publishers to the booksellers via the warehouse. Here are the definitions (and true meanings) that you will need:

RP – Reprinting (when we have enough cash).

NYP – Not Yet Published (the author/editor has not yet relinquished the manuscript).

Bdg – Binding (please be patient, we know we've some unbound sheets somewhere).

RPUC – Reprint Under Consideration (that's our story and we're sticking to it).

OP – Out of Print: a) we're not sure if it sold fast enough to reprint; b) title discontinued (we haven't told the author yet so please keep this information to yourself).

TOS – Temporarily Out of Stock (we haven't yet decided which of the above is appropriate).

Dues Recorded – We will triplicate your original order when the title is eventually in stock.

NOP – Not Our Publication (you idiot).

NE – New Edition (we got this one right).

Dealing with Booksellers

To walk safely in this jungle, you must know the animal, his lair and his habits. Bookselling is retail, but a strange kind of retail since:

• 10 out of twenty-five bookshop customers walk out

without buying anything.
- Customers take on average 12 minutes to choose each item purchased, but only 2.2 seconds to study a paperback cover.
- 52 per cent of purchases are impulse buys; only 48 per cent are planned.
- Booksellers only 'borrow' the books they offer.

In negotiating the discounts at which booksellers obtain books from publishers, a bluffer needs to bear in mind:

— That a 33⅓ per cent discount allows even the smallest bookseller a 50 per cent mark-up.

— That a 60 per cent discount provides 125 per cent mark-up (higher even than that operated by antiques dealers and the rag trade).

There are two main groups of troublemakers you should know about:

1. **Charter bookshops** – Those who maintain such good stock (they say) that they are entitled (they say) to best terms from publishers

2. **Chains** – Those who, by virtue of their high street positions and buying strength *always* get best terms from publishers.

The last few years has seen the emergence of a new-breed of chains:

Blackwell, (58 branches including George's) owned by the Blackwell family who do not regard themselves as a chain but as individual shops moving towards a corporate identity.

Dillons, including Hatchards, Claude Gill, Economists,

(100 + branches), owned by Pentos in the form of Terry Maher who took up arms against the net book agreement so it would no longer be 'heresy' for a bookseller to reduce the price of books.

Hammicks, owned by J. Menzies, with 282 Menzies branches and 29 Hammicks.

Waterstone's, owned by W.H. Smith, with 85 branches under its own name. As one sage said "If the 383+ Smith's don't beat you, Waterstone's will."

W.H. Smith

No publisher can consider his/her education complete without understanding how the Smith system works. WHS have 14 top level promotions a year based on such zingy and original themes as Back-to-School, Mother's Day, Summer Reading, etc. At the next level are the 16 'hero' promotions for mass market novels, and lastly ad hoc promotions (such as the Tolkien Centenary).

With old world courtesy, Smith's invite publishers to present their lists twice a year to 'product managers' who make the all-important selections for the various promotions. They then permit the publishers to pay nearly all the promotional costs.

Another splendid WHS opportunity is their *Bookcase* magazine. A free-to-customers bi-monthly, publishers jostle and vie to have their authors interviewed, their new titles featured – a privilege for which they will also pay happily and handsomely.

Smith's 9-tier grading system or **scale out** determines which new books go to which shops in the Smith's empire. Wise paperback publishers wait until they know what tier WHS has granted their title before pressing the print button.

Buying is almost completely centralised, leaving only 12 branches for larger publishers to blandish direct – unless you have a local interest title in which case you are allowed to sell it directly to your local branch. In general hardbacks are 'sold in' six weeks before publication, paperbacks 5 months before; and woe unto those trying to beat the deadlines.

The redesigned bookseller is likely to be young, female, and as upwardly mobile as bookselling rates of pay allow. They all have strong personal likes or dislikes e.g. martial arts, plant rights or South American Indians. All the astute rep has to do is to find out what they are and commit them to memory.

Book buyers try all sorts of tricks to avoid having to stock books at all. The most frequent is 'Business is bad' (average net profit on a bookshop is 2.8 per cent), but you should be ready for any or all of the following:

"His/her last book didn't sell very well."
"It's too expensive."/ "It's too cheap."
"Our customers wouldn't expect a book like that in this shop."
"Books on that subject don't sell in this area."
"We're overstocked in that category."
"We couldn't possibly stock it with a jacket like that."
"I think it's horrible."

Bluffers will declare that remarks such as these are only to be expected from people who are capable of saying to a would-be customer: "You're the sixteenth person I've told this morning, there is *no* demand for that book."

PLAYING THE GAME

Authors

lt is grudgingly agreed that authors are necessary to publishing. Bluffers need to be aware of the one in ten rule: one author in ten will deliver. The rest are wasting your time and theirs.

The second most important thing to know is that no author delivers on time. View very suspiciously any author who tries to. On-time delivery or close to it means one of four things:

1. The manuscript was written in the author's youth and has lain forty years in a drawer. Test by sniffing: discard the pristine front page, and go for a sample of middle pages. If you detect the lingering scent of mothballs, lavender-scented drawer-liners, or woodworm, return it at once.

2. The author has not tried hard enough. He/she is a hack, churning out vast quantities of poor quality material for monetary reward.

3. Nobody else will touch them so they have time on their hands.

4. He/she is a pervert.

Authors may be divided into two categories: live ones and dead ones. Some live ones do admittedly appear more than 50 per cent dead but because of the rules on copyright and the public domain, it is worthwhile running a check on their status.

If authors are of the live variety, they divide into two kinds: those who are members of the Society of

Authors and The Writers' Guild and those who are not. The ones who are, are Trouble. They know their Rights. They will argue terms and conditions rather than simply sign their contract and melt away into the night, suitably grateful. They will haggle over serial rights in Czechoslovakia, cartoon rights in New Zealand, and may even mention **MTA**s. They will demand signing sessions in towns where neither you nor they have enough relatives or friends to make a respectable showing. They will alienate booksellers in a fifty-mile radius going in and asking for their books.

The best author of all is the one who is third rate and doesn't pretend to be anything else. He or she will accept your publishing decisions with appropriate deference and keep out of the way.

Here are a few points to making life easier

1. Even the greediest of authors can be sweetened by receiving complimentary copies of their book translated into an unintelligible language. This gives them a tremendous buzz.

2. With the author's six free copies to which they are entitled on publication (now more often ten) send a note headed 'Why your book will not be on sale at Didcot Station or Wittering-under-Marsh News-agents and Tobacconists to the Gentry'.

3. Presentation-bind a copy of the book just for them.

Communicating with Authors

This takes four forms: lunches, telephone conversations, letters, silence. Most of your letters will be apologies: for taking so long before acknowledging receipt of their manuscript, for taking so long to give them a decision, for taking so long to send along the contract, for taking so long to send the advance, for taking so long to publish, and so on. Authors do not seem to realise just how busy publishers are.

Some helpful phrases to smooth publisher/author relations include: "This merited serious consideration" (I couldn't face looking at it for weeks); "It's not quite right for our list" (either we don't publish children's books or we wouldn't be seen dead with this); and "Our programme is full for the next ten years" (your manuscript is simply unpublishable).

The rejection letter is an art form, polished rapidly by the vast quantity you have to send out. You might choose to emulate John Maynard Keyne's two-edged approach: 'Thank you very much for sending me a copy of your book which I shall waste no time in reading.'

A glance at the letter accompanying most manuscripts will instantly reveal the author's illiteracy and general unworthiness of your time and attention. Brighten up Monday morning or ease the pain of a hangover by rejecting half a dozen out of hand.

On occasion, expressions of regret may be perfectly genuine. If you think the book is publishable, but not by you, pass it on to a friend who can. Then two people owe you.

The author's unforgiveable sins

1. To deliver a long manuscript of loose unnumbered pages. When reassembled, you will find you have one page left over.
2. To send you a compatible disk which loses all fractions, accents and punctuation in its conversion.

Agents

Agents are the unashamed 'bookies' in the sporting world of publishing. When George Bernard Shaw's Mr Pinker ran off with all his money in the 1930s, this merely served to substantiate publishers' view that agents were a bad thing, parasites on the work of others, and not to be trusted. Now, they are viewed as a necessary evil. The less kindly still omit the word 'necessary'. A post-war phenomenon, these canny middlemen (usually women) may be considered the true entrepreneurs, turning a fast buck and spotting the next deal while their hand still tingles from the last one struck and shaken on. 140 or so are listed in *The Writers' & Artists' Yearbook,* but you need to know at most half-a-dozen – and three of these should be good.

Like publishers, agents too have their 'backlist' of solid sellers, often the estates of the dead authors where for 50 years there are large sums of money to be made from rights and reprints.

Who Looks After the Dead and Famous

A.P. Watt — P.G. Wodehouse, Somerset Maugham, Robert Graves

Peters Fraser & Dunlop — Evelyn Waugh

Lawrence Pollinger — H.E. Bates, Scott Fitzgerald, Graham Greene, D.H. Lawrence.

Eric Glass — Jean Cocteau, Jean-Paul Sartre.

Ed Victor — Raymond Chandler, Irving Wallace.

The type of author reveals quite a lot about what you may expect from the agent. There are fuddy-duddies in agenting as well as in publishing.

With English as the almost-universal language, authors working in English have a vast market for rights available to them, with tidy commissions for their agents. Agents are therefore great rights-splitters and hagglers. No nice blanket deals for them. They will tease apart every last strand – TV rights, film rights, merchandising rights – and negotiate a separate deal on each. When both the author and the agent have a track record, be on guard as the agent talks-up the asking price. The downside, from the agents' point of view, is the handholding, brow-mopping, and other distasteful tasks that fall to the nanny.

Many best-sellers are agent-driven (read also market-driven: agents are at the sharp end and know what the market wants). Manuscripts may be commented on, even substantially revised by an agent. It is said that Carol Smith looks after her authors to the point of helping them write their books.

Auctions

Auctions are tremendous fun and you should get involved in as many as you can. They follow a splen-did ritual, almost a courting dance. The selected pub-lishers will only be given ten days in which to make up their minds, which they do by telephone or by sealed bids. Once a **floor** is established with **topping rights** (as in "she had established a £50,000 floor but had to use her topping rights to beat off Pan"), the auction can gain in momentum. This is probably a hard/soft deal so the mighty funds of the paperback houses will be brought in. It will also include an

override; a **pass-through clause**, an **option**, and an **escalator**. By the time you are au fait with these terms you should be much poorer.

Bidding need not be on a full manuscript; it can be on a synopsis and samples, or if you've got a big name, just the title will do. There are lots of early contestants but as the figures rise, the numbers fall. Then it becomes a battle between the keen and the desperate.

Contracts

You need to remember one main thing about contracts: the person with more muscle uses theirs.

Most companies have standard contracts with only a few blank spaces for manoeuvre. This is as well. Editors who do not understand the financial realities of publishing may find they have given away their whole year's profits and control of production to a fast-talking agent or a very sharp author.

If you don't have a standard contract, don't let any old lawyer draft it for you. It should be created by someone versed enough in these matters to produce something watertight that protects your rights.

The negotiable areas you need to be wary of are the royalties, the amount and timing of the advance (on signature, on delivery and/or on publication), and the various subsidiary rights. The rule to remember is if it will be good for the author it will be bad for the publisher.

Note: Publishing talk always omits the thousand. Sir Robert Lusty's cable buying rights to Svetlana Stalin's memoirs stated 'Fifty and not a penny more'.

Rights Terms:

The rights business is awash with jargon. You will need to know enough to convince your listeners that you move in the right circles. Here is a selection.

Buy in – Bought on one side of the Atlantic and published on the other, simply reproduced by photography. A fast form of publishing, it avoids re-writes, lunches, editorial overheads, and contact with the author. This explains why so many books on English publishers' lists are of American origin. And vice versa. Computer scanning makes the process even easier, but muddies the financial water putting offset fees under dispute.

Pass through clause – When rights income is handed over within thirty days, as opposed to the more usual six or nine months. Resist this one at all costs as it will affect the half of your business which is holding on to other people's money.

Override – Apparently generous gesture to authors in which they get prompt payment of paperback rights income. (But you will have agreed a side deal publisher-to-publisher.) Less prevalent with today's hardback and paperback editions coming from the same house like a meat factory producing steaks *and* sausages.

Pre-empt – An agent's way of getting the most out of a publisher without the expense of an auction, and your opportunity to make your top bid. When this isn't enough, you resort to:

A floor – Supposedly your top bid. But always include topping rights in case your judgement is wrong.

Topping rights (expressed in percentages) – What you have to resort to if another publisher gazumps you.

Step-up deal – When the percentage of the paperback rights increases if you a) appear more than x times on *The Sunday Times* bestseller list; b) sell more than y copies in the first year; c) film rights are sold.

Escalator – Generous gesture from a publisher when sales exceed a fixed number.

Option – Notoriously valueless clause allowing the publisher first look at the author's next work. This no longer means you can pay the same as before, but should preclude having an auction.

Foreign Rights

To make money at publishing, international sales are essential. Here are a few points for bluffers:

America

When dealing with Americans, bear this fact in mind: Congress at one stage had to decide what would be the official language. English defeated German by only four votes. Any country which needs to vote before deciding on English as their official language has to be foreign.

The great thing about Americans, as someone once said, is not that they are so clever, but there are so many more of them. Americans do read. But most of them read for business, for weight-watching, tax evasion, Aids avoidance, and vicarious sexual pleasure. The largest bookselling chains in the states, Barnes & Noble/B. Dalton and Walden Books, generate sales in the region of one billion dollars from roughly 1,750 branches. America therefore offers a vast, lucrative market (or dumping ground) for British publishers' products. Unfortunately, they return the compliment.

New York is where the biggest sums change hands and the biggest print orders are committed, where the auctions happen, and fortunes are made or lost in a day. The most venerable American publishing houses used to bow to commercial reason with an office in New York but maintained their literary and social stature by operating out of Boston. Today, only one (Houghton Mifflin) remains. Many of the most profitable publishers now have offices in the Mid-West or on the West Coast. Clearly, face-to-face negotiations will be essential with these firms.

Business in New York is frenetic and also has to be done in person. Time your visit so that it is:

a) not too long - New Yorkers are impressed by one who has ostensibly come for 48 hours
b) not over any Jewish holiday
c) not before any big fair such as Frankfurt or the ABA.

Timing is crucial. New York publishers have two speeds only – panic and becalmed. You must catch them on the first tempo, when they think they have no books for the Fall. Then they'll buy anything.

And make sure the European Community remains an exclusive market for you since imports into the UK of American editions of your books cannot be stopped through the courts.

India

There is only one reliable Indian publisher. Find him. As for the rest, no matter how adamant they are about wanting to buy your books, if you send samples to India you will simply be making a present of them.

Japan

Whether you go to Japan or not, the rewards are enormous. There are 9 million undergraduates in Japanese Universities. As a result there are masses of Japanese publishing companies – well over 4,000 at the last count. Most British publishers save themselves the difficulty of dealing with them , or with the swarm of competing agents (not to mention lukewarm sake and paralysed knees) by using an exclusive agent. Happily, learning Japanese will give you no better deal than they do.

China

At some point in the future, China will sign the Berne Convention, or its equivalent, and join those nations who pay to produce books even if it's in Mahjong sets. Another good opportunity for the sale of foreign rights. As Noel Coward pointed out, 'Very big, China.'

Eastern Europe

The situation here is complex and chaotic. There are no guidelines, except don't give up. And never cold-shoulder anybody: they might be the powers that be publishing-wise next year. Simply everybody is maintaining a watching brief.

France

Do not expect to sell rights to France. This fiercely Anglophobic nation labours under the misapprehension that literature actually began on their side of the Channel. Their books are as different as their business cards which are always twice the size of anyone else's, and won't fit in your wallet.

Australia

This should now be considered a foreign country: it has adopted copyright laws which make any title not published in Australia within 30 days of its English language publication anywhere else in the world, in the public domain. The Australians read more cook books than any other nation. We're not saying anything else as we want to be first in the field.

Piracy

In Taiwan, Iran and South Korea, and until recently in comprehensive schools in England-north-of-the-line, the use of the photocopier or photolitho printer has meant that publishers and authors have been cheated of many millions of revenue. It is unlikely that the majority of your publications will attract the attentions of the average Taiwanese pirate, who tends to go for simpler propositions such as photocopying the *Encyclopedia Britannica*, but you might as well know about it.

Book Fairs

Rather like the financial futures markets, at a book fair you trade in properties that do not yet exist. Five and six figure sums are promised for rights in as yet unwritten books, purveyed with immense confldence by other people who have already spent money on securing them.

Their purpose is to display their wares – hundreds of thousands of them – in this international market place, to buy and sell rights and, even more importantly, to confirm old contacts, re-heat recent ones, and establish new ones.

Frankfurt

Over 8000 publishers from around 90 countries descend on Frankfurt each year. Comfort yourself with the fact that no-one who claims to be an old hand is genuine if he/she cannot recall:

a) wading in wellingtons through the mud from Nissen hut to Nissen hut in the early days

b) staying in a brothel by mistake.

The international bestseller is born at Frankfurt as buyers light their torch from the originating house and, or so they plan, set the world alight.

One of the delights of Frankfurt is the 'Diagram Group Prize' for the discovery of the Oddest Title. Notable entries have included The University of Tokyo's *Proceedings of the 2nd International Workshop on Nude Mice*, and HMSO's *Physical Properties of Slags*.

The rules are basically:

1. Never do a deal at Frankfurt. No one expects you to buy a book and, if you do, it will only end in tears. The only people to do deals are novices not yet immune to 'Frankfurt fever', show-offs and remainder merchants.

2. Instead, be seen to participate in auctions. With a few useful phrases, you can join in happily without spending any money. (See Rights.)

3. When playing the game, never suggest a bid so low that you're not taken seriously, or so high that you are taken too seriously. Very experienced Frankfurt hands have actually managed to get their floor on the table, but this is a tricky stunt that bluffers would be advised to avoid.

4. Never read anything at Frankfurt. If you like it, you may want to buy it – always a mistake. And if you don't like it, why waste your time?

Also remember that:

1. The two topics of conversation of all-consuming interest are:

a) where you are staying, and

b) where are you eating tonight.

This is not because the enquirer is interested in your welfare, but rather in his own. Really good hotels are hard to find, and most food at Frankfurt whether Indian, Italian or 'International' tastes of pig fat.

2. No oral agreement made at the Fair is worth the paper it's written on. Talk, unlike the food and drink there, is cheap. Duck the food queues by eating amongst the even-more-impoverished Eastern Europeans.

3. A diary full of appointments is an essential requirement. By using several coloured pens you can give the impression of being thoroughly sought-after when in fact only those in, say, red, are real.

4. If you have been over-enthusiastic, you may need to explain that you've sold the same rights to two different buyers. The way out is to declare that both have secured bidding rights.

5. You may at some point in the proceedings, feel the need to look sober when smashed. The solution is easy. Stand next to a printer.

6. The person you elbowed out of the taxi-rank last night is guaranteed to be the person you have to face on your first appointment the next morning.

7. Everyone is bluffing.

ABA

Every year on Memorial Weekend (so that small booksellers can shut their stores without fear of losing business) the American Booksellers' Association has a conference in one of a select band of cities. The ABAs are so regular and crucial that one can date events from them as in "We shook on it in Anaheim; he reneged in Washington."

Intended as a forum for American publishers to show their wares, the ABA is now invaded by numbers of Europeans. You will inevitably spend the greater part of your time touting to booksellers who order, some six months later, two copies, post-paid.

London

At the London International Book Fair you find yourself going round in circles or figures-of-eight, seemingly unable to break out. Only Hodder people know where they are: their large corner site hoves into view at every turn.

Do not permit the hordes of unknown faces to undermine your confidence. A sizeable number constitute the entire staff of publishers' London offices crowding in for a day out.

Avoid Booksellers' Day filled with tweedy provincials, and double-check where your chosen seminar is. Ill fortune might detour you instead to the Mills & Boon "How-to" with its red roses of romance.

The variety of watering holes provides a challenge. Return visits for 'important' meetings should be to the champagne bar, even if the main topic of conversation is still 'What's the London Book Fair really for?'

It is vital to show your face here, to prove you're still alive and in business six months after Frankfurt.

Bologna

The civilised version of Frankfurt, but only for Children's books. Primary colours and balloons festoon the stands. But not all is fantasy. Publishers are heavily concerned with contemporary themes: lesbian mothers and gay fathers, and how not to catch Aids when kissing better a cut knee.

Unlike other fairs in Bologna, this is the only one when the prostitutes go on holiday.

How to Get Started on Your Own

There are three basic routes:

1. Acquire a backlist of existing titles. These will go on selling and providing income while you build up your own list.

2. Acquire world rights to a title which is destined to be a mega-selling success.

3. Identify those titles which are already out of copyright which are worth re-issuing, and you have a ready-made list. If you can get away without having to have the whole thing re-typeset, you're definitely winning.

The small press offers scope for trying out new things, and giving page-space to even your craziest interests, so long as they're legal. It also meets the needs of the publisher who wants to keep control and stay involved in every aspect of the business, i.e:

a) those who are pathologically incapable of fitting in when someone else is running the show

b) those who won't delegate.

One of the secrets of success is new technology. Using that effectively, a couple of creative people can produce about ten books a year, in modest quantities, and make a living from it.

The greatest problem, it is generally agreed, is distribution. You can do it yourself, repping and delivering your own books to the bookstores, but most end up being distributed by someone else. From then on it's simply a question of musical chairs.

What to Publish

The publishing game is still sufficiently chancy for the wildest risk. Here are some kinds of water not all over fished, where you might cast your fly:

1. Autobiographies of future Prime Ministers, Archbishops, Leaders of the Opposition, Speakers of the House of Commons, Multiple Murderers, etc. A sharp eye for potential is essential here.

2. Absolutely any Television Programme. The benefits of publishing spin-offs from the screen are so wellknown that it is difficult to get in here. Most large publishers now have someone almost permanently assigned to tie-ins, bidding for properties or persuading TV producers to serialise books. But there are a few little chinks left.

3. Vanity Publishing (in the best possible taste). An

alliance with a rich institution can be most useful. The problem here is simply one of establishing the 'right contacts'. Many of them, like the BBC and the Getty Museum, do their own publishing, and nothing can be done about it, but the bright bluffer might consider approaching museums and suggesting they do their own guide rather than leaving it, and the good pickings, to private companies.

4. Bizarre and Out of Use Languages department. There is no subsidy as solid as a government subsidy. With ethnic minorities being all the rage, it shouldn't be too difficult to revive. For example, there are 40,000 Cornishmen living in the Bronx, and they need a break.

5. Education. With the invasion of the video, the copying machine and piracy, schoolbook publishing in the UK is not in a good way. Far better would be to launch into foreign markets where English is a saleable commodity.

6. The Works of Famous Authors, e.g. Rudyard Kipling. Even if the famous works of the famous have been in print without cease, it is always possible to publish a collection of their lesser known but equally genial pieces of journalism, with an introduction by, say, the Editor of *The Times*. People of this ilk positively adore being asked to write an introduction.

7. Series. These save everybody time and thought. The author and the editor have to do a little bit of thinking, but the salesforce doesn't – and the booksellers love it because they recognise and identify

sameness with relish. There is not a bookshop in the land, however humble, that does not stock and sell Ladybird Books, Observer Books, Teach Yourself Books, Made Simple Books. This sort of publishing is the bread and butter of the book trade. If you cannot find original material for a series, you can always look around other publishers' lists for titles which are out of print, and acquire the rights.

8. Books on Subjects Dear to a Few People's Hearts. Not everyone owns a Hispano Suiza, but those who do, have done, or wish they did, might buy a book on the subject. Ditto patio gardens, oleographs, china bananas. There are only a few categories you might wish to avoid:

a) pornography – videos have taken over
b) books for the educationally subnormal – there are too few of them
c) books on alternative medicine – there are too many of them
d) anything to do with computer software, nuclear warfare, or historical biographies, unless about Nelson.

Packaging

Packagers believe they are the only truly creative people in the publishing world today. Never disagree with them. You may have need of their services one day, or you may find yourself becoming one.

To play this game, you need to have an idea for a book (genius) then produce a dummy (cash), and hawk it around to find someone willing to invest in it (stamina). This you do internationally (see Frankfurt and America) until you have enough money to start on the project properly – and to subsidize the flights/phone calls/exotic lunches necessary to have got it this far in the first place.

There are two rules:

1. Publishers never keep to schedules, but you are expected to keep to yours.

2. If it can go wrong, it will.

How to be Acquired

There is no limit to the number of times you can sell your company. But for your first sale, you are pristine, impeccable and unsuspect. There is nothing reprehensible about this sort of carry on. For publishers to sell themselves many times is more standard than rare. If you don't like the results, or look back on the financial knife-edges with nostalgia, or simply want to start the process all over again (especially now you've got the money to do it), you might try to emulate others (André Deutsch, Paul Hamlyn, Carmen Callil, Anthony Blond) and buy yourself back.

Those who have been taken over by non-publishing people should watch the new brooms with some indulgence. History has shown that publishing does not operate by the same laws of the universe as industry, despite the fevered attempts of many an industrial mogul to force it into that mould. The rule, if you are part of such a take-over, is sharpen your image to fit in, look eager, sound enthusiastic, and wait for them to give up. They will.

Then, with luck, you can either fix a management buy-out, or be acquired by another publisher. Even the most variegated list has some sort of attraction. The large publishing organisation will have a warehouse, a set of travellers, a London or provincial office (or both), and the enormous overheads that this operation engenders. It will always be hungry for turnover.

A high proportion of this can be produced in-house, but this leads to more expense. Editors, sub-editors, their assistants, production departments, art departments, publicity and promotion departments, plus the managing director's secretary and the marketing director's harem all cost a lot because they employ human beings. Any proposition which involves the injection of more turnover without over-head must be welcome.

Accounting convention makes it cheaper in the long term to buy a backlist than create a new one. The goodwill acquired in the acquisition can be written off, as can losses against the profits of the acquiring firm. Your product therefore can be put in with theirs at no additional investment in human beings, except yourself. (Do not undervalue yourself. This means employing somebody else to negotiate. You are worth more than you think, and such opinions are beter expressed by someone other than yourself.)

An excellent strategy is to achieve the sale and then be so awkward that your owners have to buy you out. This leaves you free, and financed, to start all over again.

GLOSSARY

General Terms:

Book – What publishers say they produce. Covers a multitude of sins.

House – Where publishing happens, the company or organization. Abbreviated form of 'work-house'.

Privileged presses – Ones who are allowed to print the Bible.

Advance – Cash overture. Usually half the earnings due to the author on the first printing. Less, if you can get away with it.

List – A publisher's programme, either seasonal (as in 'Spring list') or historical ('Ah, it was a great list').

Author – One who believes there is money in books.

Publisher – One who proves that there isn't.

PA (Publishers Association) – The publishing industry's whipping boy.

BA (Booksellers' Association) – The Godfather of the book trade.

IPG (Independent Publishers Guild) – Association of publishers too poor to pay the PA membership fee.

SYP (Society of Young Publishers – Contact club for the young hopefuls.

WIP (Women in Publishing) – Support group for females with advancement in mind.

MTA – Minimum Terms Agreement, the least an author can be offerered by a publisher.

Net Book Agreement – a) That which booksellers believe prevents them from huge book sales; b) publishers' attempt to maintain control after books have left their hands.

Editorial, Print and Production Terms:

Setting/typesetting – The process of converting ideas to reality.

Proofs – Evidence that something's happening.

Galleys – First attempt by publishing slaves at making the typescript legible.

Face/Typeface – Type design of your choice, e.g. Bembo, Bodoni, Baskerville.

Fount (USA **font**) – Complete set of same typeface and point size.

Point – Unit for measuring size of 'body' of type. 72 to the inch. 0.0138 in. (in UK & USA); 0.0148 in. in Europe). Trust them to be different.

Em – Space occupied by a letter 'm' in any particular typeface and point size; so called because 'm' is the widest letter of the alphabet. Good word for Scrabble.

En – Half the width of an em.

Ennage – A collection of ens. The number of characters on any width or depth of a page.

Folio – Grand name for page number.

Cast-off – Calculating the number of pages a certain amount of copy will make when set in a certain typeface to a certain area.

Bleed – When the image goes up to the cut edge.

Orphan – The first line of a paragraph which is the last line on the page.

Widow – Single line or word at the top of a page. Considered undesirable.

Erratum slip – Too important an error not to point out.

Dummy – Blank book, or non-productive editor.

Postlims – Padding (i.e. advertisements for other books) at the end of a book to fill pages.

Prelims (USA **mechanicals**) – Pages that get in the way of getting into the book. For precise etiquette see Butcher.

Butcher – Copy editor's Bible. Compiled by Judith Butcher of CUP.

Hart's Rules – Printer's oracle. Horace Hart's *Rules for Compositors and Readers*. Now in its 39th edition.

CRC (Camera Ready Copy) – Critical final stage of typesetting. Never really ready.

Ozalids (USA **blues**) – The all-film-together copy of what is heading for press. Last chance to catch mistakes.

ISBN (International Standard Book Number) – Reference system begun in 1967 when people didn't have so much to do. 10 digits in four groups:

Group 1 – Country of origin
Group 2 – The publisher
Group 3 – The book itself, its edition and binding
Group 4 – The check digit to pick up errors in the other 9.

Estimate – Printer's guess. Allow a percentage for 'extras'. Contingencies should take care of the rest.

Plant costs – Unavoidable basic costs – e.g. typesetting, colour separation, platemaking.

Variable Costs – Costs which invariably increase, e.g. paper, print, binding.

Perfect binding – Imperfect method of glueing pages to the cover. Cracking a spine to test if a book is perfect bound is a nice way to show off your expertise and annoy booksellers. Use their stock.

Imposition – Printer's equivalent of a paste-up. Arrangement of filmed pages before platemaking in the correct order for printing and folding.

Finished copies – Stage when the sales department become convinced all editors are mad.

Marketing Terms:

Legs – What a book should have, i.e. Will it walk out of the shop?

Campaign – Tour of local radio stations.

Advertising – That which serves to prop up a) the sales of a book already selling; b) the ego of the author.

Review copy – Additional income for members of the press.

Chat-show – Show hosted by a personality who has a) not read your book, and b) will prevent the title or publisher being mentioned.

Embargo – Prohibitory order by publishers ignored by the press if the book is at all interesting.

POS (Point of Sale) – Promotion material sent to bookshops and put out of sight.

Counterpacks – Expensive display boxes kept under the counter.

Spinners – Rotating stands which you pay for and other publishers use.

Dump bins – Origami obstructions in bookshops.

Discount – Booksellers' profit. Never considered enough.

Subscription – The number of copies ordered by the book trade prior to publication. Usually equivalent to the total sale after returns.

Returns – Gone today, here tomorrow.

Single copy order – The bane of the book trade. Time consuming, unprofitable and usually cancelled the day after despatch.

Cyclical delivery – An excuse for publishers to go round and round in circles, say every Tuesday.

On consignment – The method by which publishers lend books to bookshops and hope to be paid when unsold stock is returned.

Sale or return – The method by which booksellers have the automatic right to return unsold books and receive credit.

Firm sale – Arrangement by which booksellers pay for the books they order. Last heard of in 1928.

THE AUTHOR

Dorothy Stewart (ex Fincham, née Miller) burst onto the publishing scene as a cub reporter on Scotland's top weekly, *The John O'Groat Journal*. Literary ambition drove her to Aberdeen University, from which she emerged with a degree in Sociology, a certificate in part-time youth leadership and joint authorship of a paper in forensic medicine. Spurred on by this success, she went to West Africa to learn how to be a publisher.

When she returned to Britain she found that her ability to spell most African names was a saleable commodity, and joined Macmillan Press.

She transferred from the Gentlemen to the Players to run McGraw-Hill's UK business management programme, and ultimately back to the gentlemanly atmosphere of the Institute of Chartered Accountants as Publications Director. During this time she became more interested in business than in bluffing, even acquiring an MBA and finding a hidden talent for financial management. These she has now invested in her own business, writing, ghosting, and watching the publishing scene with bemused benevolence.

THE BLUFFER'S GUIDES

Available at £1.99 and (new titles* £2.50) each:

Accountancy	Marketing
Advertising	Maths
Antiques	Modern Art
Archaeology	Motoring
Ballet	Music
Bird Watching	The Occult
Bluffing	Opera
British Class	Paris
Champagne*	Philosophy
The Classics	Photography
Computers	Poetry
Consultancy	PR
Cricket	Public Speaking
The EEC	Publishing
Espionage	Racing
Feminism	Secretaries
Finance	Seduction
Fortune Telling	Sex
Golf	Small Business*
The Green Bluffer's Guide	Teaching
Hi-Fi	Television
Hollywood	Theatre
Japan	University
Jazz	Weather Forecasting
Journalism	Whisky
Literature	Wine
Management	World Affairs

All these books are available at your local bookshop or newsagent, or can be ordered direct from the publisher. Just tick the titles you require and send a cheque or postal order (allowing in the UK for postage and packing 28p for one book and 12p for each additional book ordered) to:

Ravette Books Limited, 3 Glenside Estate, Star Road, Partridge Green, Horsham, West Sussex RH13 8RA.

Prices and availability subject to change without notice.